SYMMETRICAL UNIVERSE

Adult Coloring Book #1

Mandalas and Symmetrical Images for
Relaxation, Inspiration, and Stress Relief

by Stephen Pitts

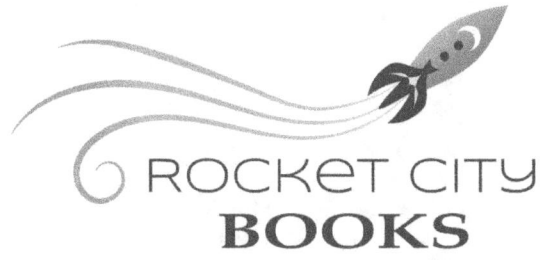

ROCKET CITY
BOOKS

www.rocketcitybooks.com

Published by Rocket City Books
PO Box 74
Taft, TN 38488
info@rocketcitybooks.com
256.714.7980
www.rocketcitybooks.com

ISBN 978-0-9903547-1-0

WELCOME!

Welcome to the Symmetrical Universe Mandala and Symmetrical Images coloring book! I hope you enjoy contemplating and coloring these complex symmetrical images.

I drew every image in this book with pen and ink on 14x17 or 14x14 paper. My drawings are all done by hand, using fine tipped Rapidiograph pens. The way my process works is first I use a ruler and a compass to generate a pencil line grid. Once the grid is in place I then draw the designs in ink. The images are randomly generated and sometimes change significantly during the process of creating them. The drawings are created by drawing one symmetrical feature at a time, much like growing a crystal.

The Mandala drawings are inspired by my interest in Hinduism, Hatha Yoga, Indian mysticism, floorplans of European cathedrals, as well as my interest in crystallography. My drawings are an expression of the inherent beauty found in symmetrical structures. I began drawing mandalas while attending Indian Springs School in Helena, Alabama in the 1970s. My first mandala drawings began as simple experiments requiring a few hours to design. This eventually led to the more complex designs which required 80 to 100 hours to complete. Some drawings are abstract geometrical designs. In others, I have tried to incorporate archetypical symbols and shapes similar to Rorschach patterns which may invoke a variety of conceptualizations to viewers of my artwork.

Tibetan mandalas have provided much of the inspiration for my mandala drawings. I have also found much fascination with the artwork of the Celts, especially the Celtic knots which I have incorporated into a few designs. I have also tried, in a small way, to emulate M.C. Escher, whose work is quite enigmatic. The majority of my drawings are done with black ink, although some have been re-drawn in color.

In this book, each section includes an original drawing which may be too detailed to color. The following pages are all more detailed images of sections of each drawing for you to enjoy and color. If you are interested in coloring an original drawing in the original size, order a print from www.symmetricaluniverse.com.

To get the most out of this book, I recommend using colored pencils fine-point markers, and gel pens. Before you color on one of the drawings, use the test section on the very last page of this book to test your coloring pencils, pens, and erasers. Check to see if your pencils or pens look nice on the paper and make sure they don't bleed through to the back.

To see more of my drawings, visit my webpage at www.symmetricaluniverse.com. You may order prints of any of my drawings in a variety of sizes. You may also order my other coloring book on mechanical and steampunk designs. Sign up for my newsletter to get updates about new drawings, new coloring books, and a schedule of my art shows.

Thank you for ordering this book. I hope you enjoy it!

Steve Pitts

BYZANTIUM

"Knowing yourself is the beginning of all wisdom."

~ Aristotle

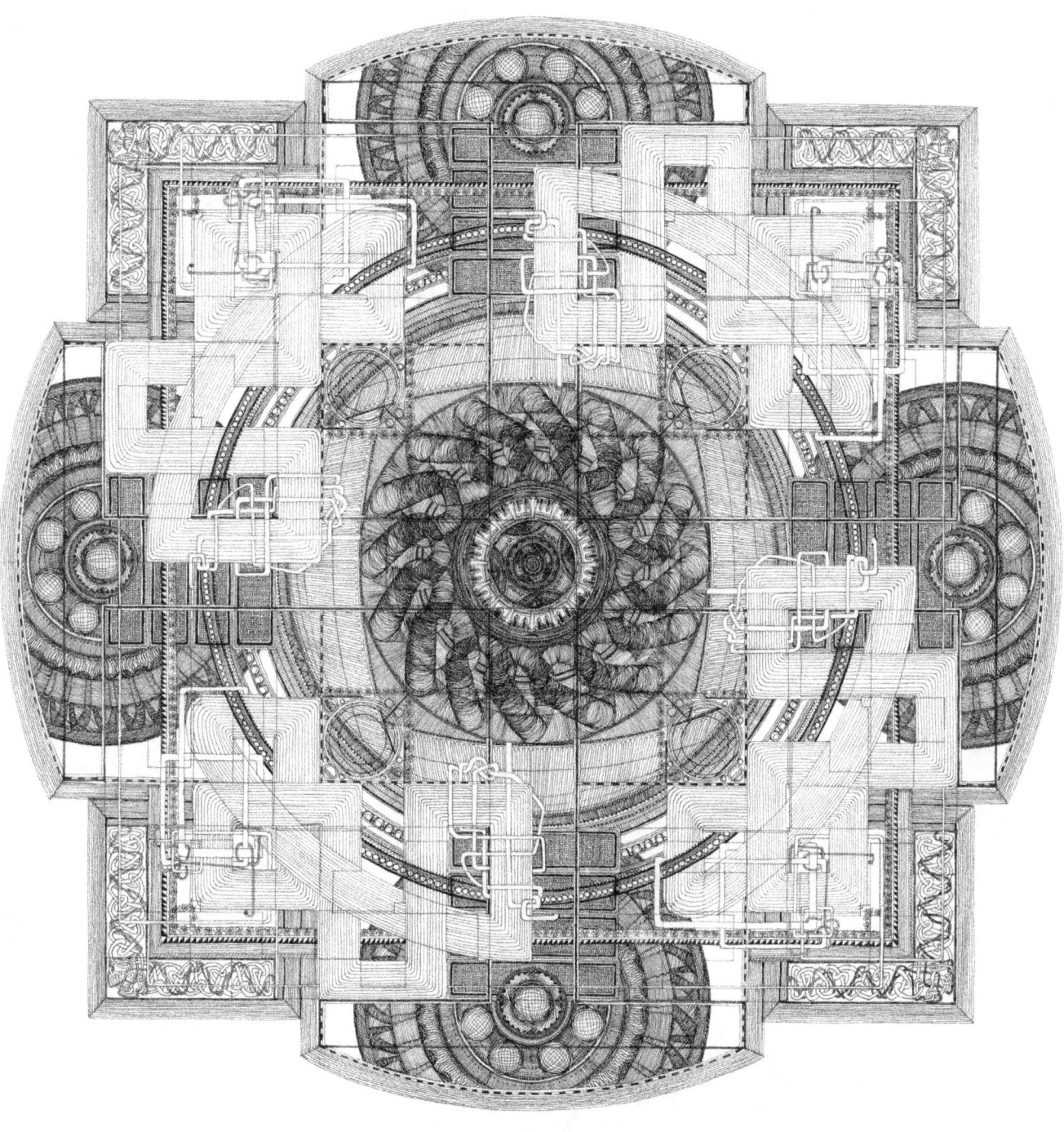

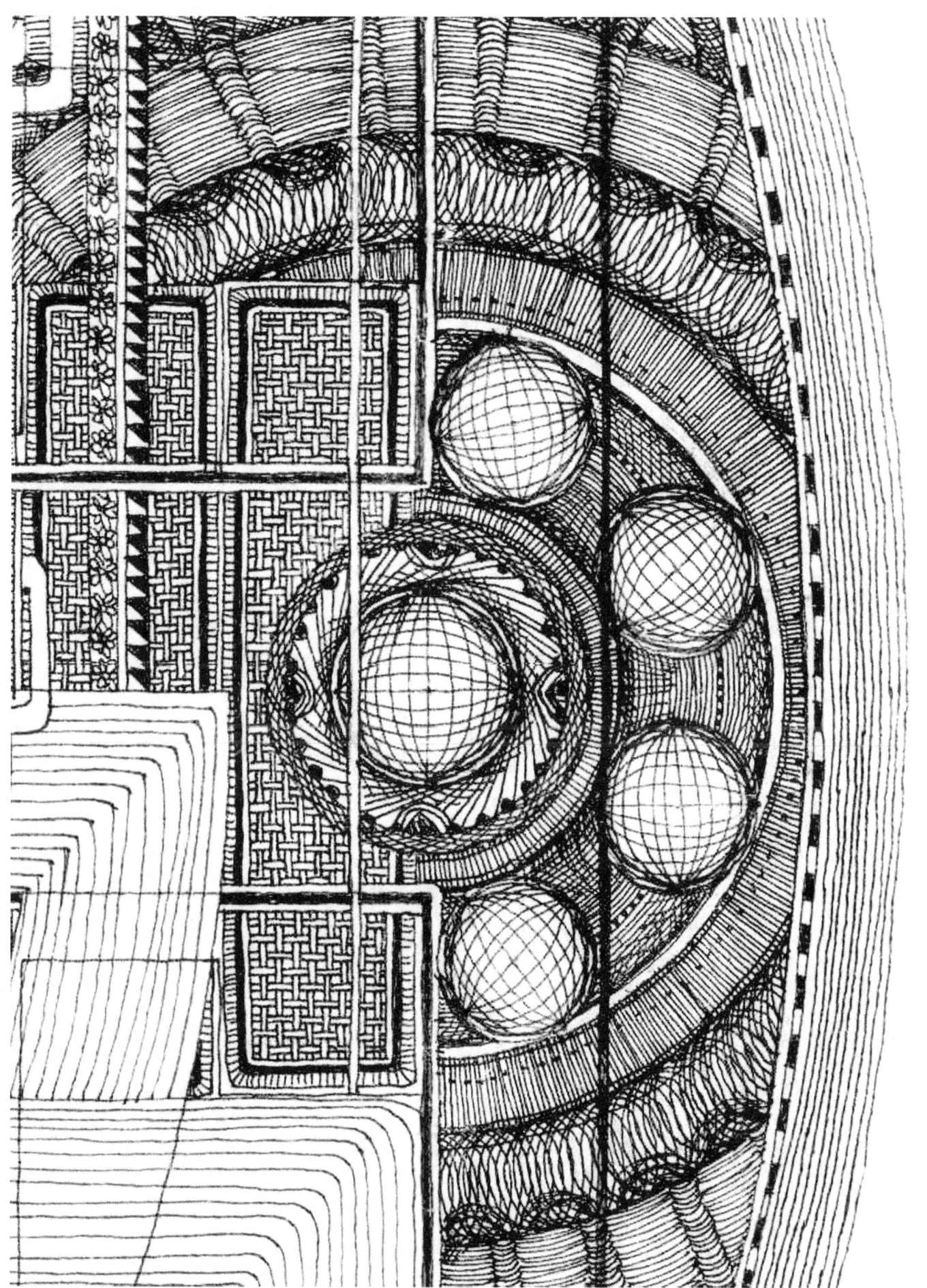

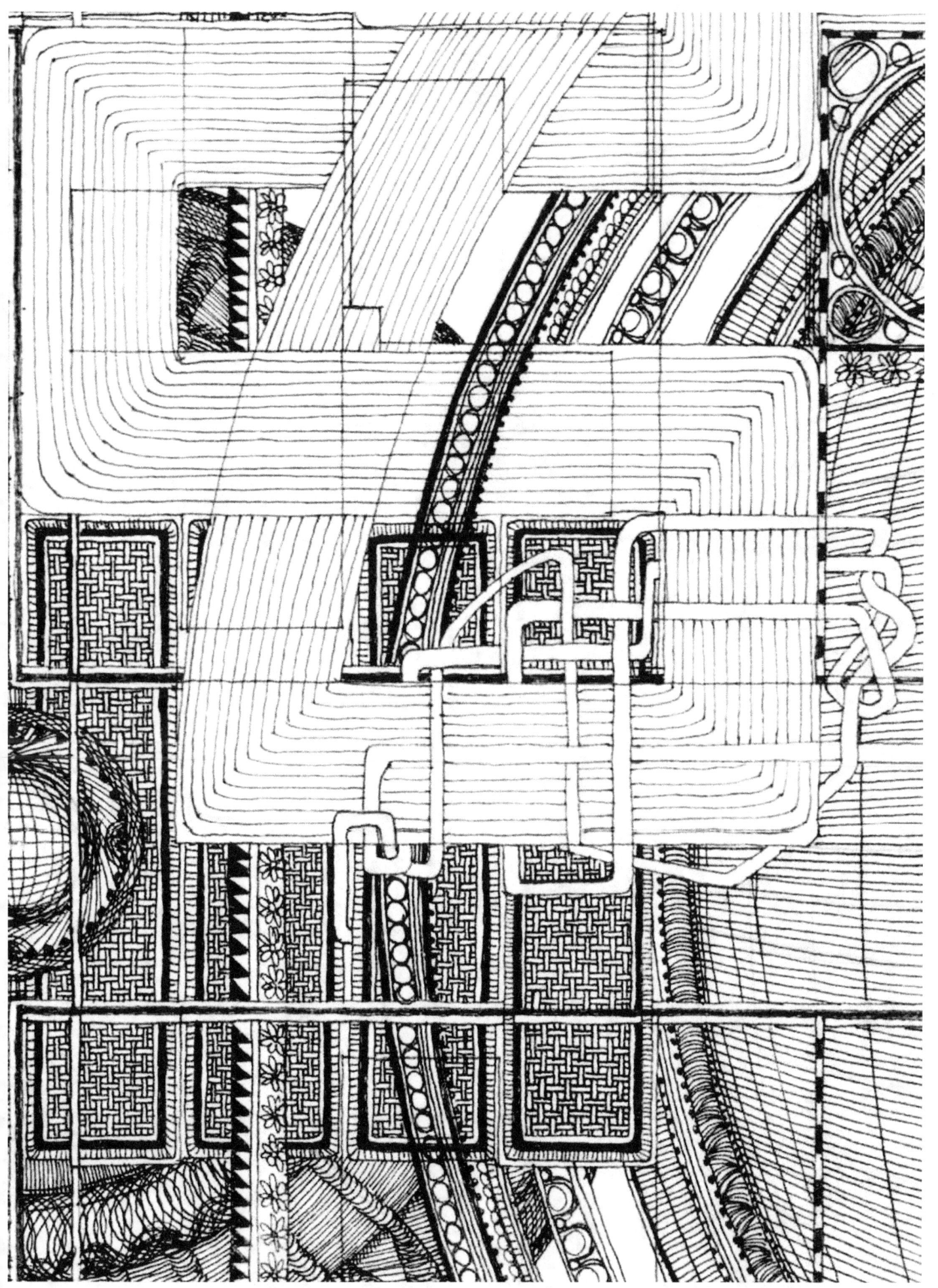

SPHERES

"Nature is an infinite sphere whose center is everywhere and whose circumference is nowhere."

— *Blaise Pascal*

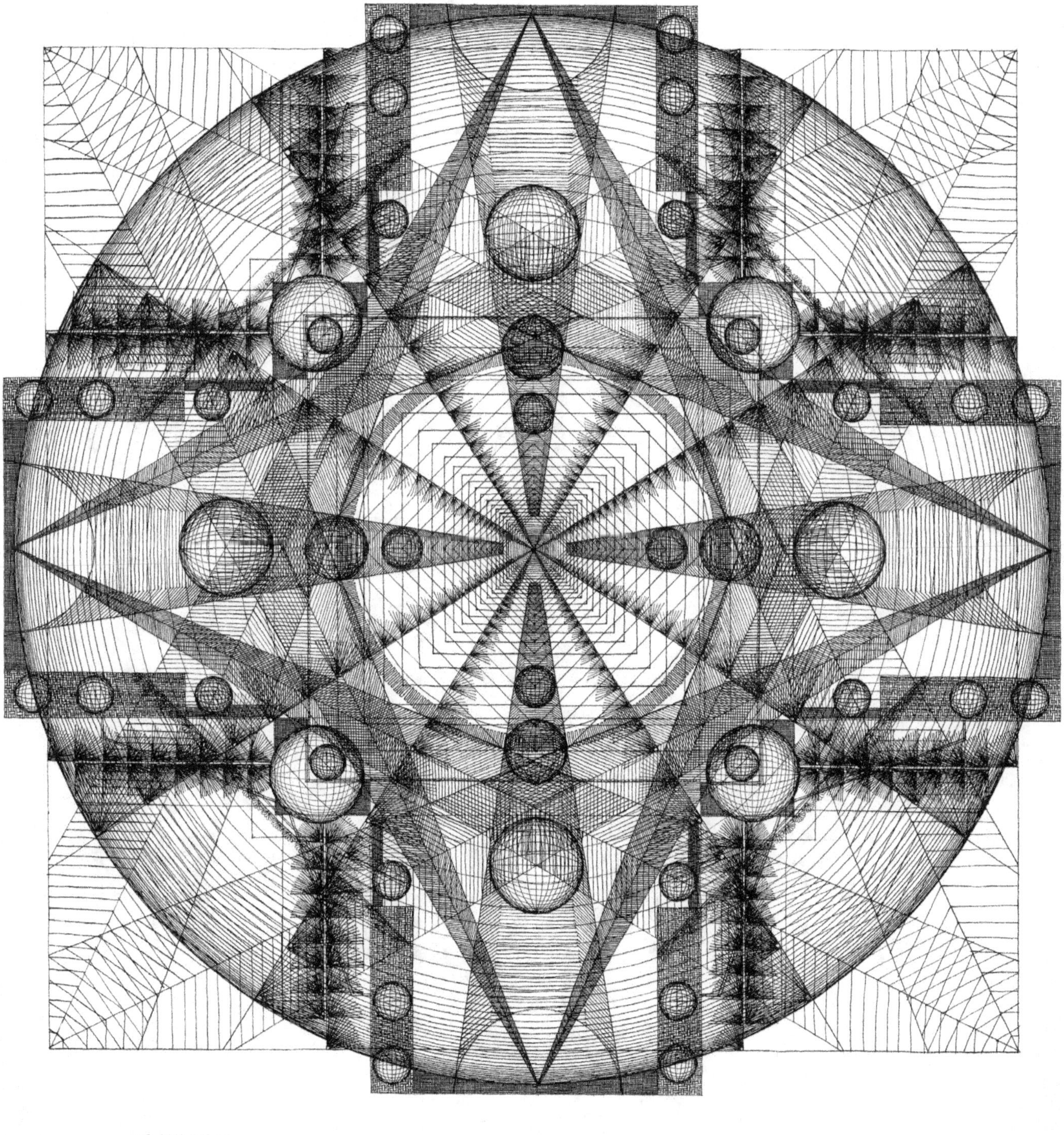

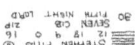

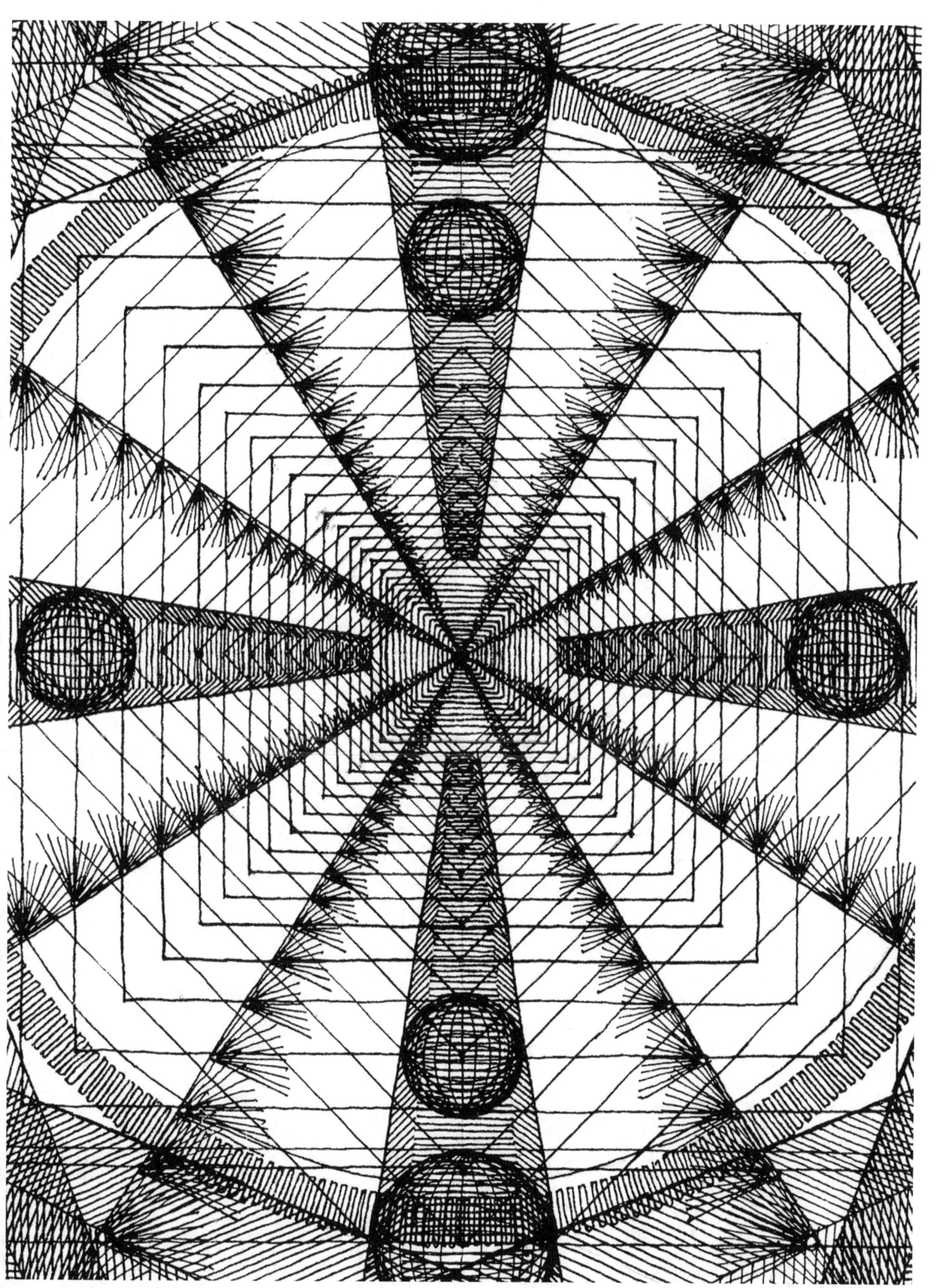

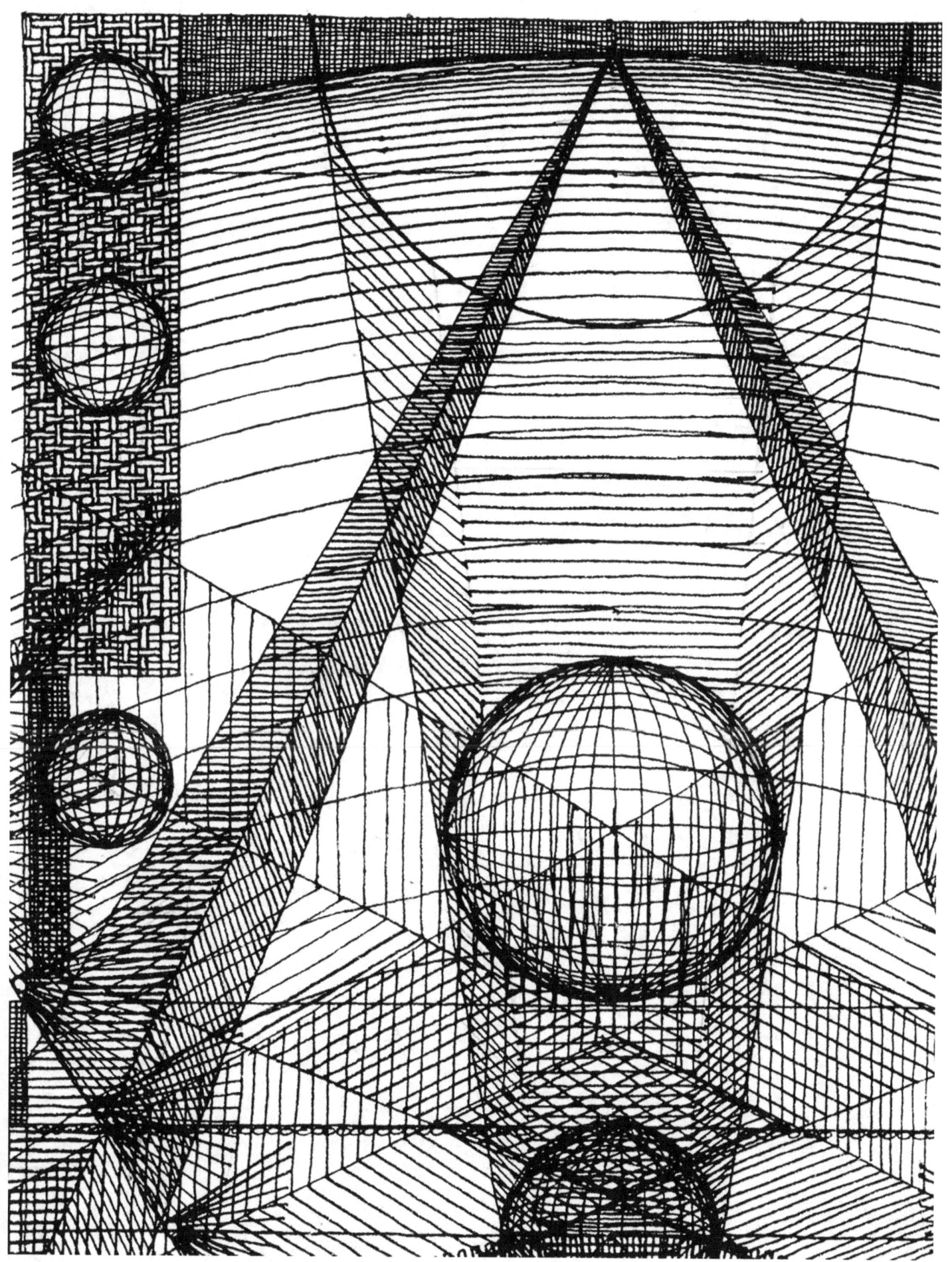

TIBETAN MANDALA

"Thousands of candles can be lighted from a single candle, and the life of the candle will not be shortened. Happiness never decreases by being shared."

~ Buddha

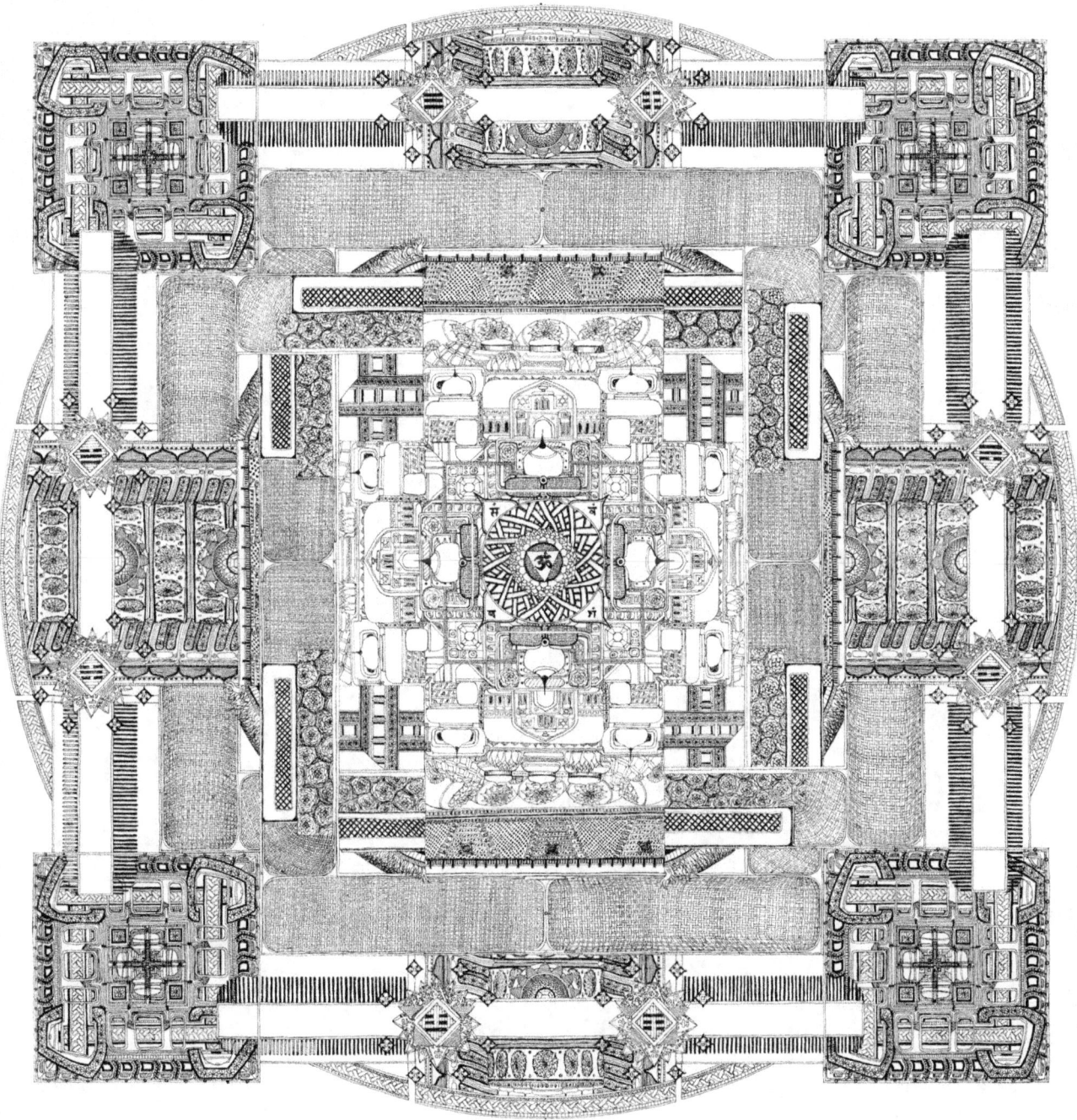

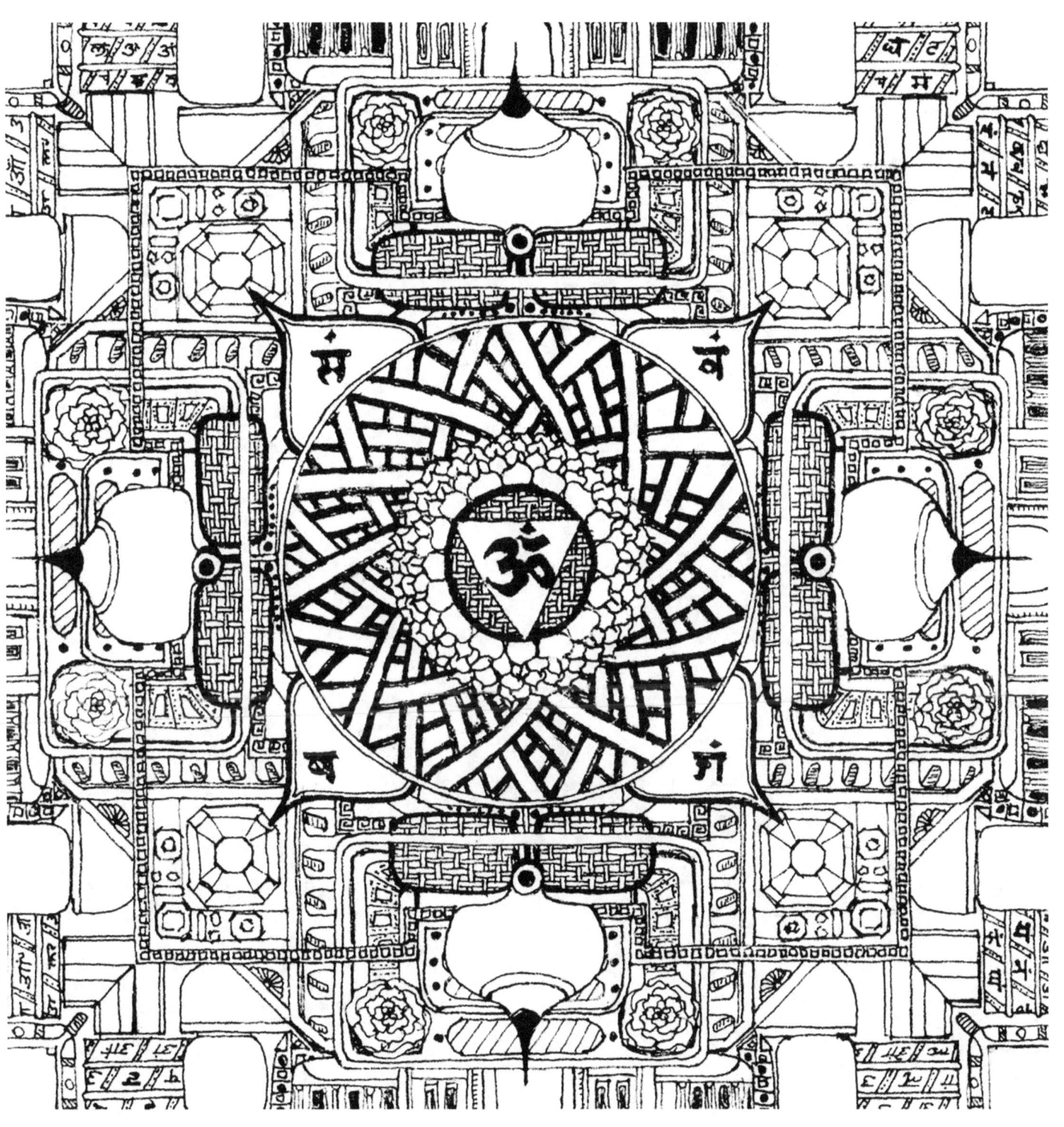

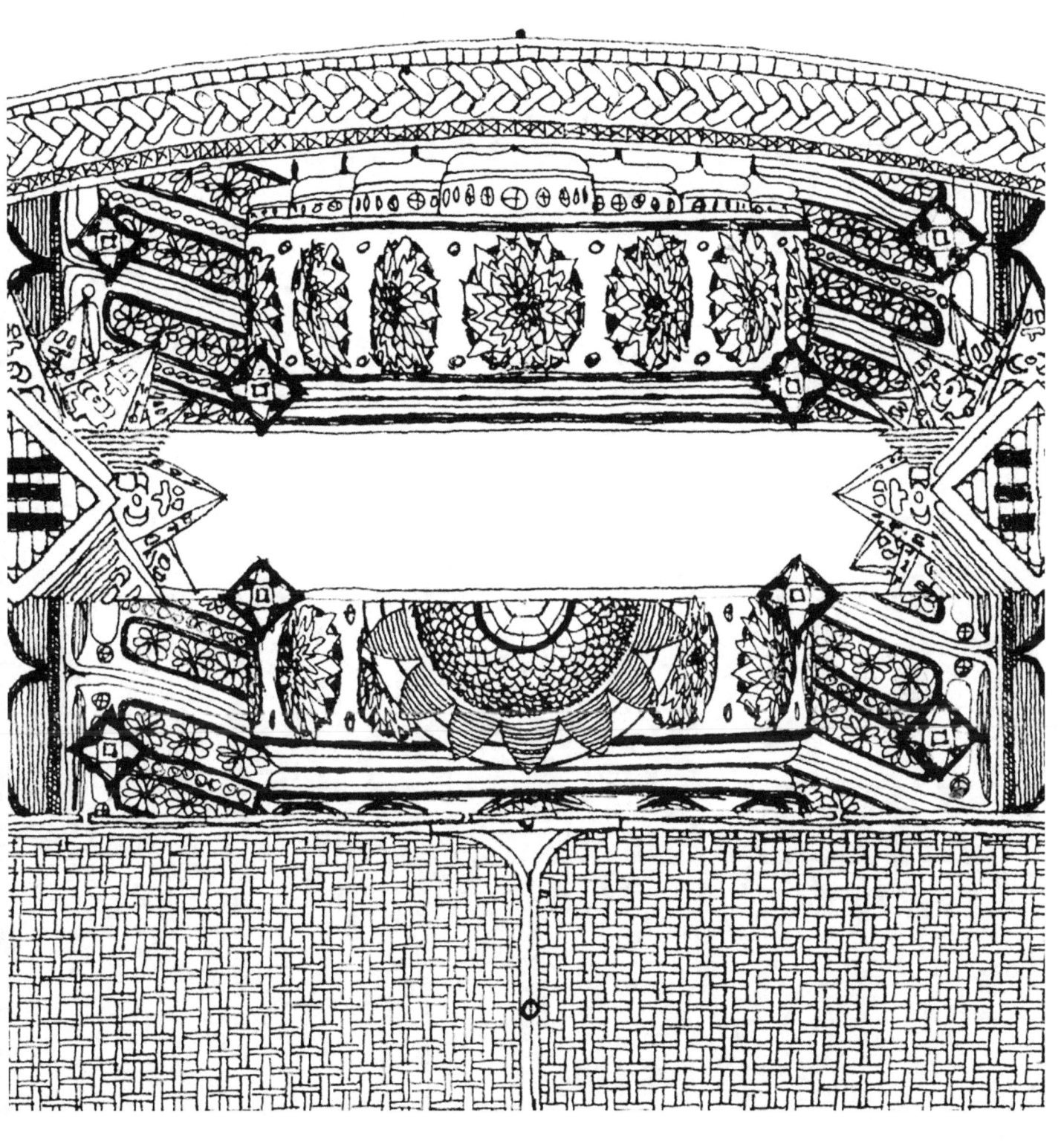

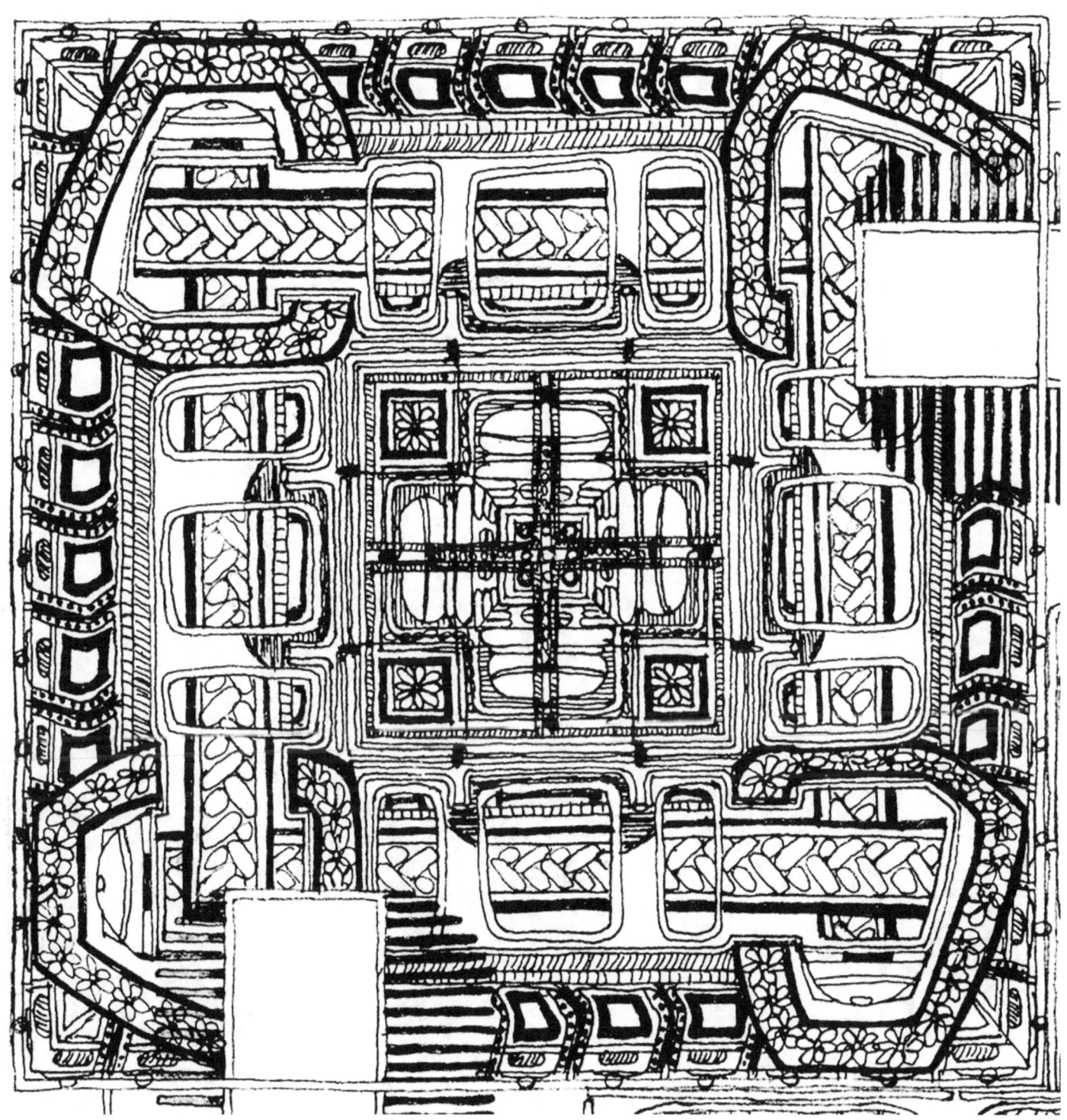

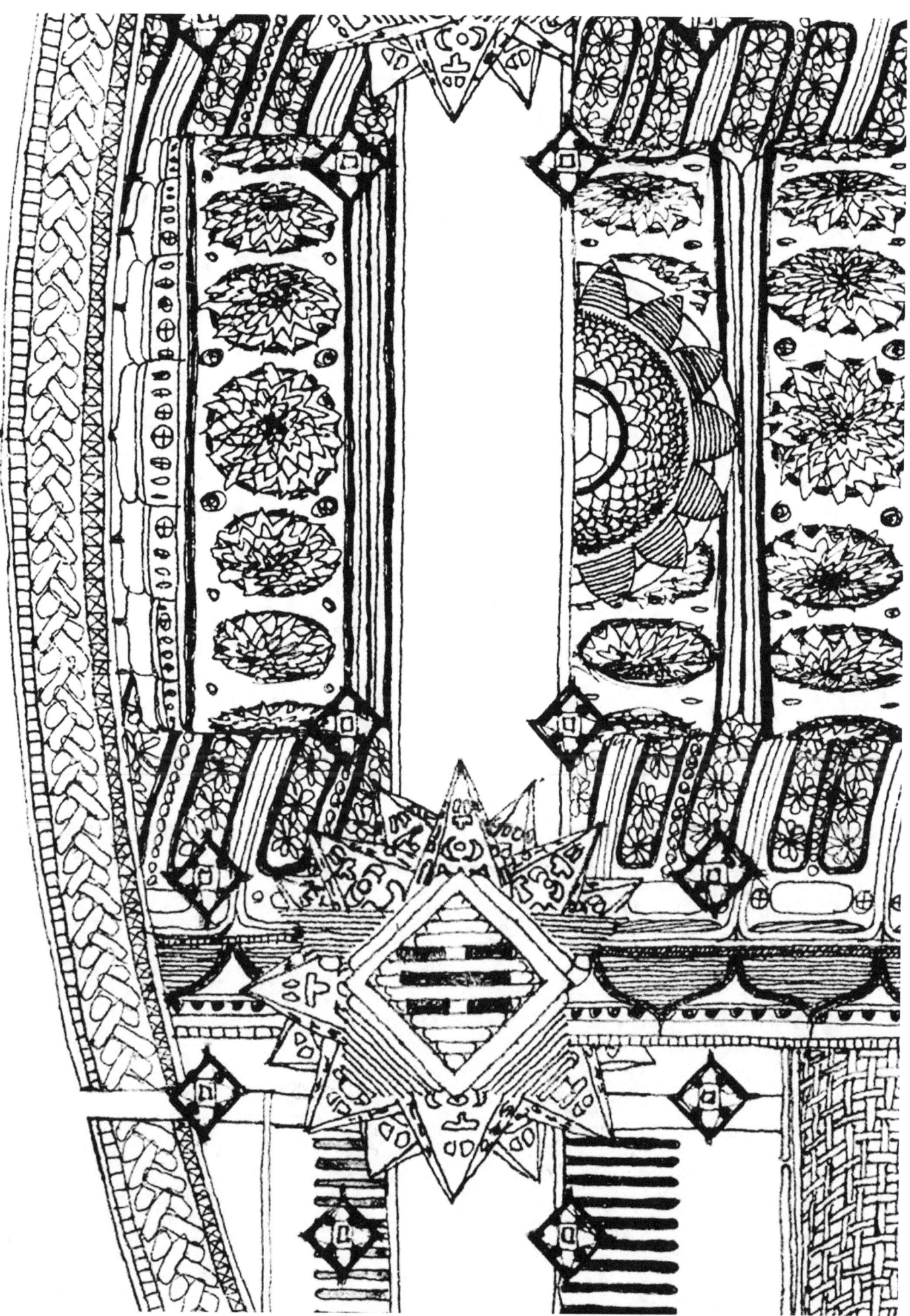

AZTEC SWASTIKA

An ancient symbol dating back at least 12,000 years, the swastika represents good luck, prosperity, and eternity to Buddhists and Hindus.

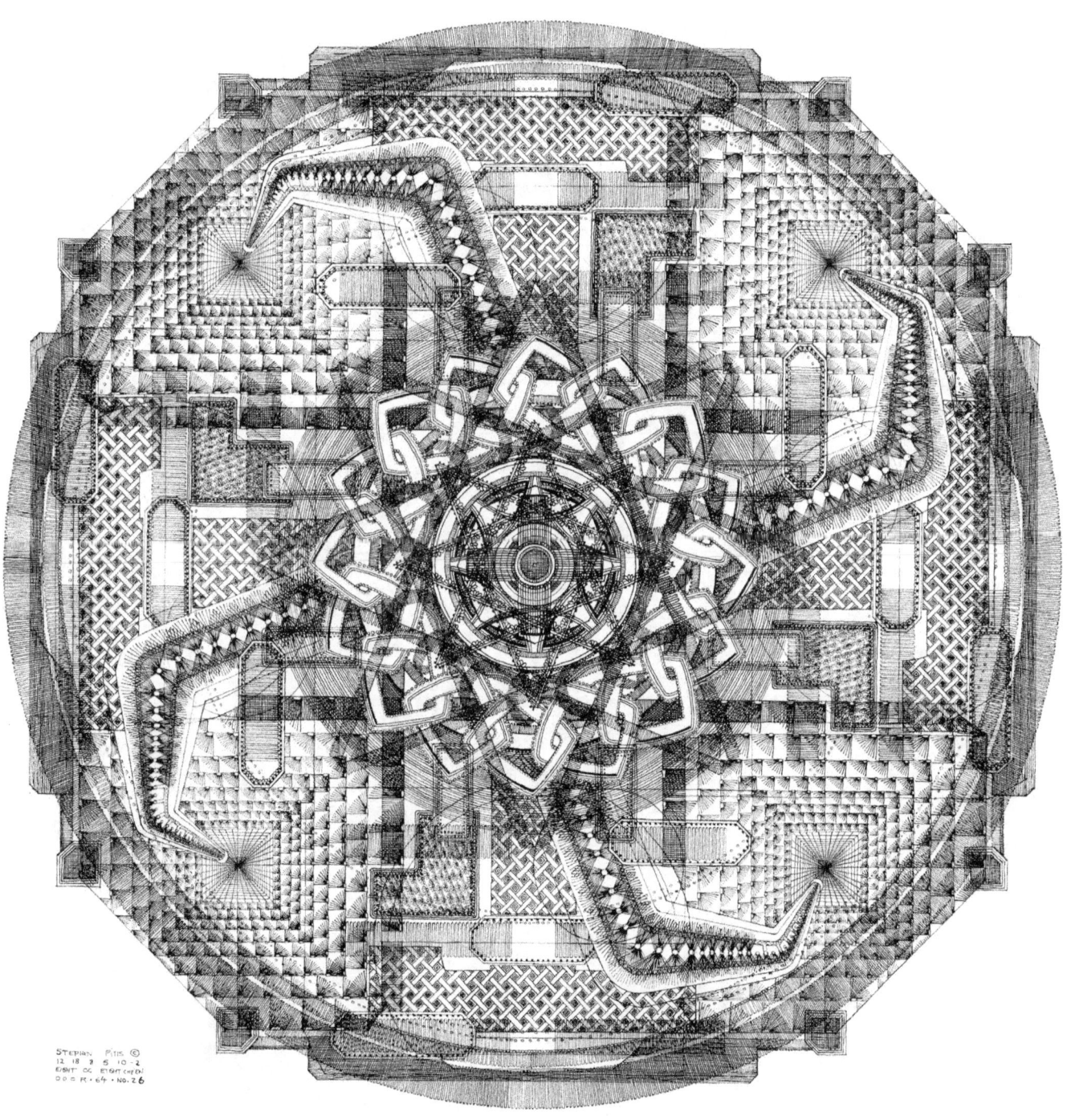

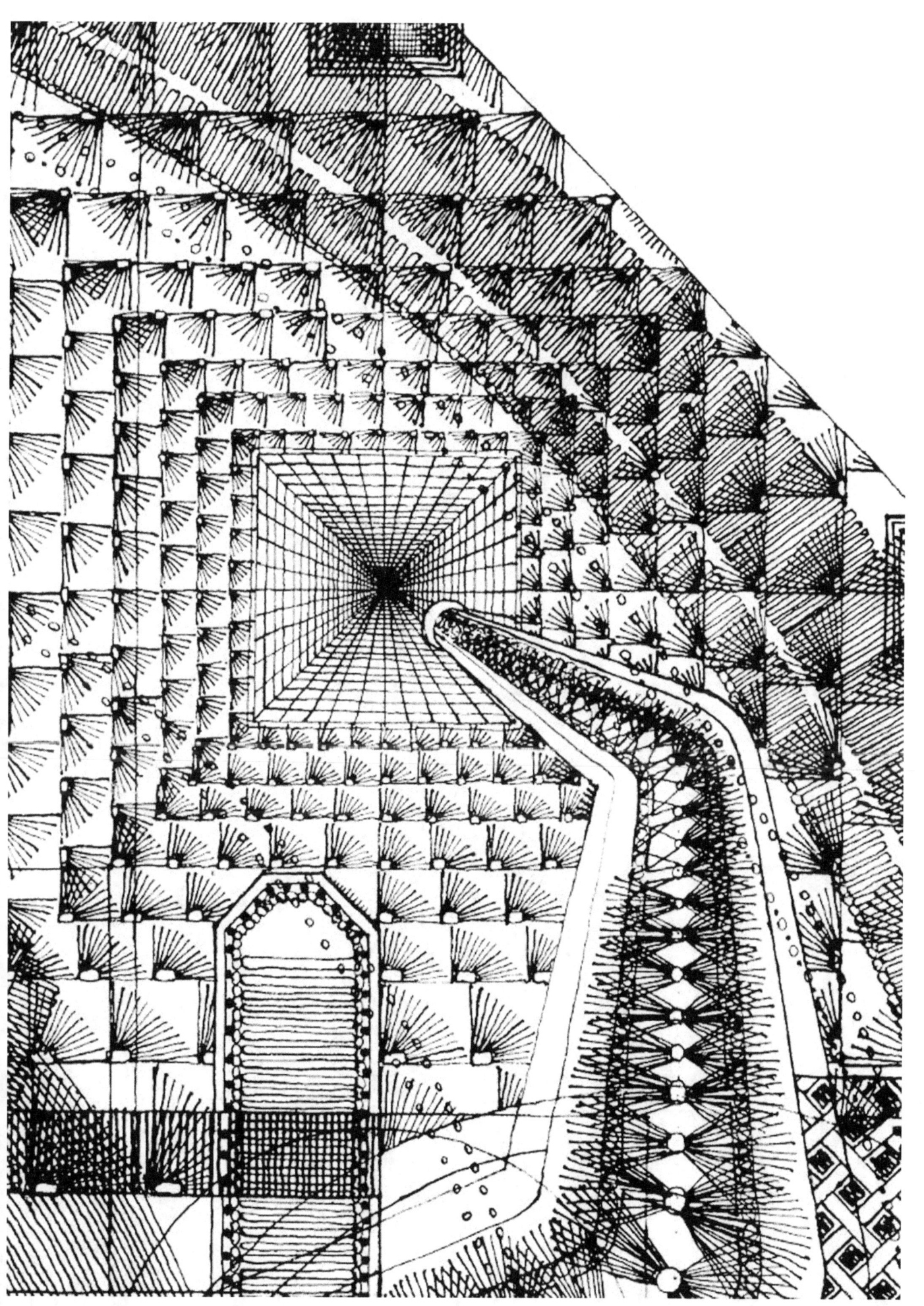

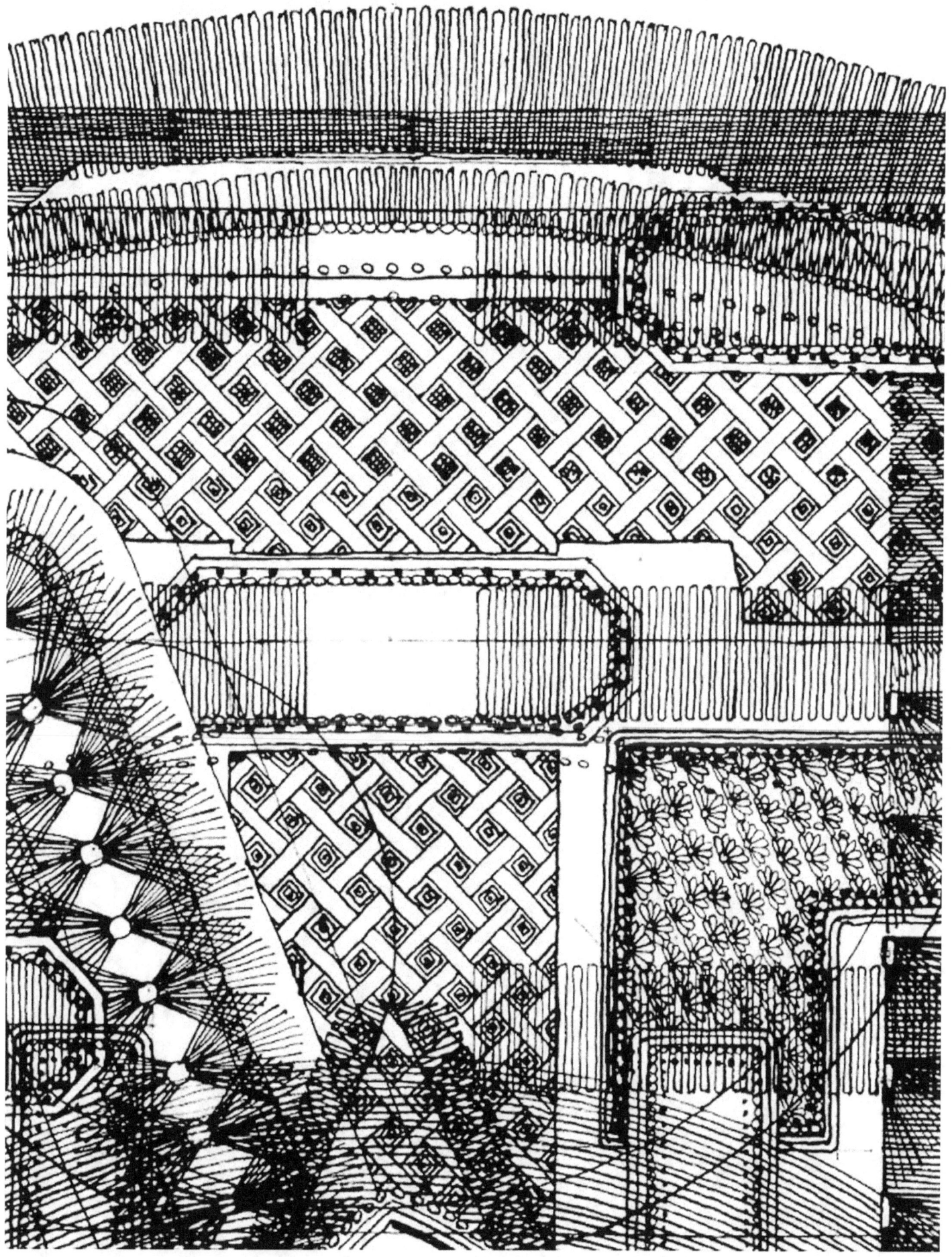

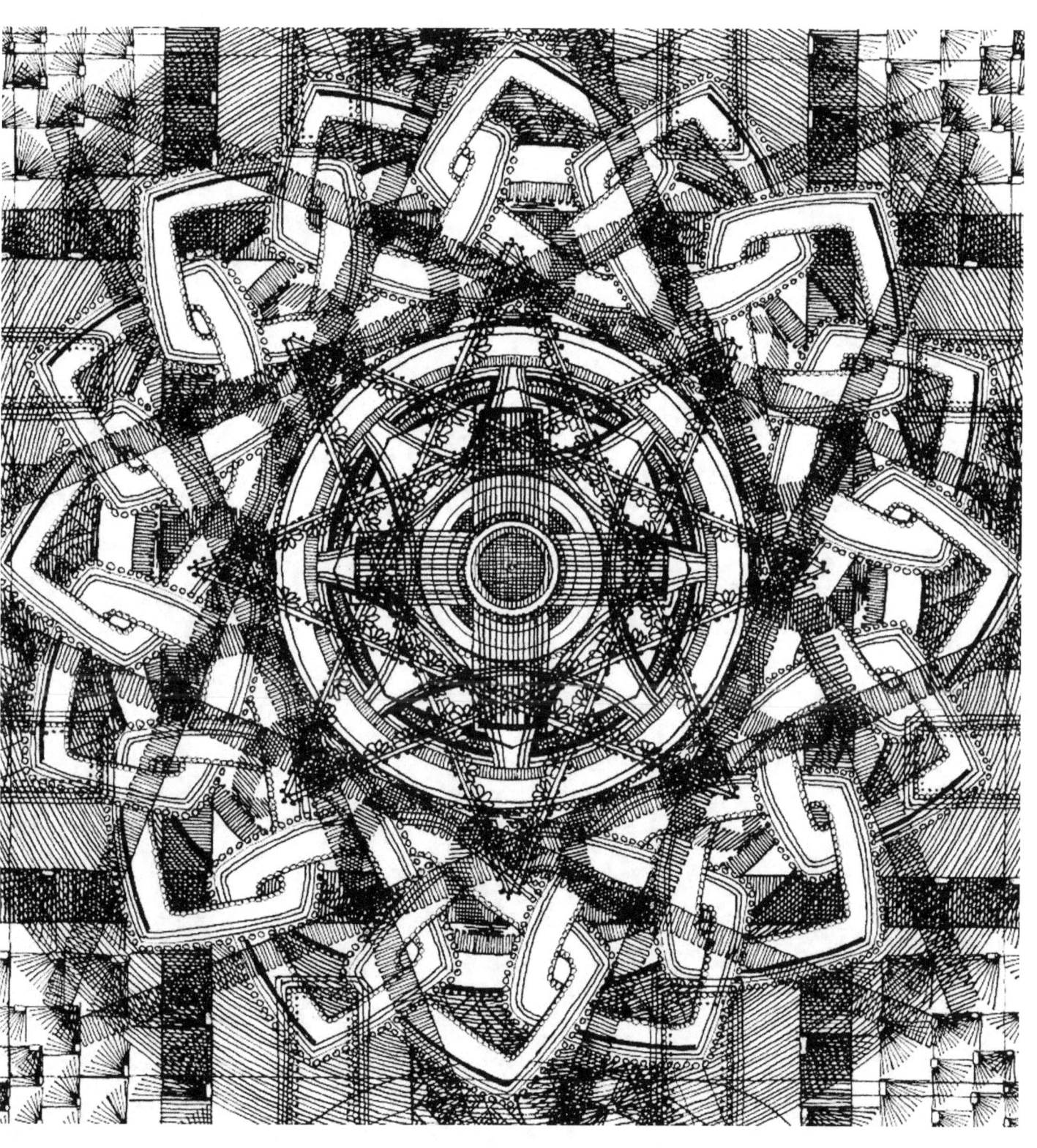

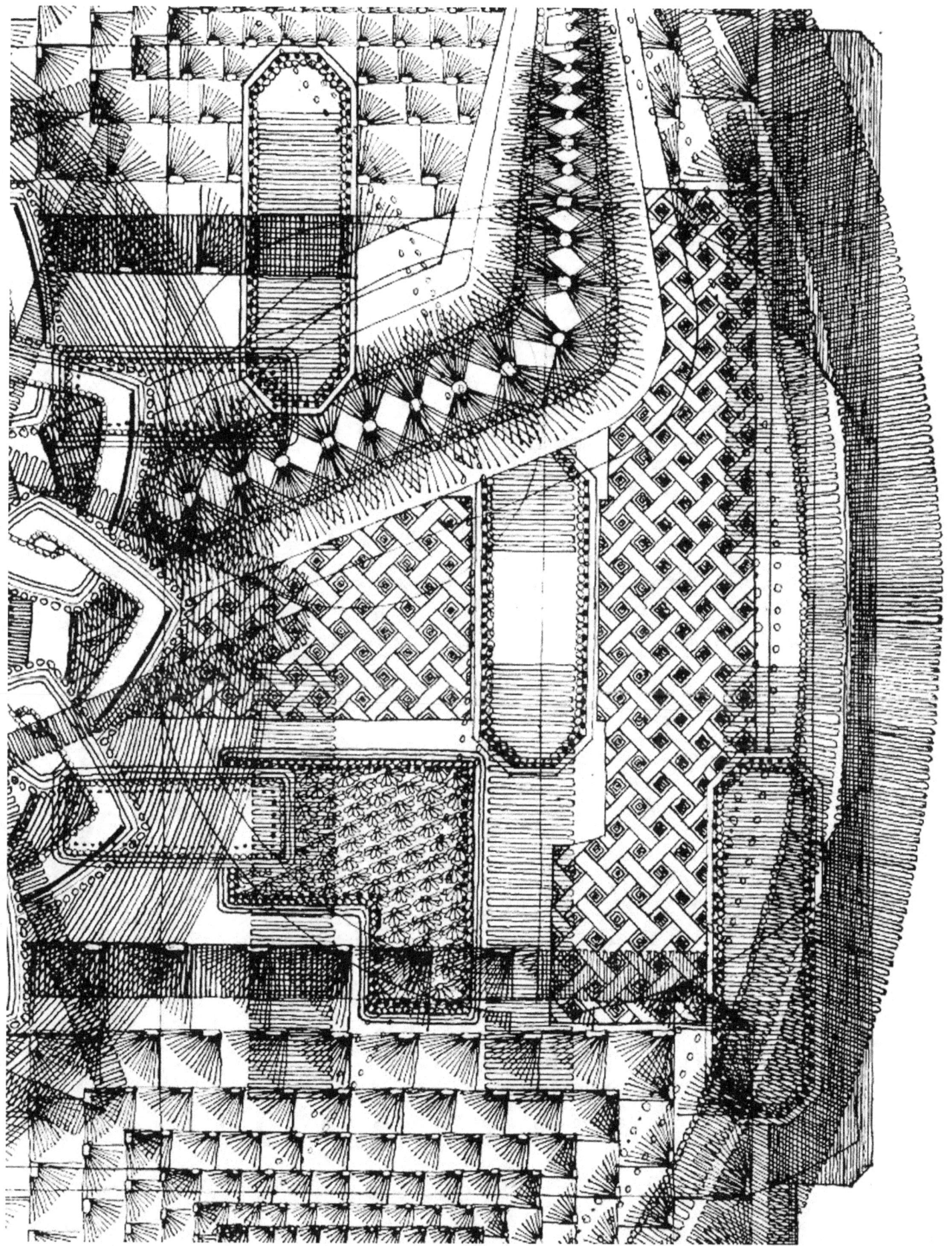

ROPE WHEEL

"The wheel is come full circle."

~ William Shakespeare

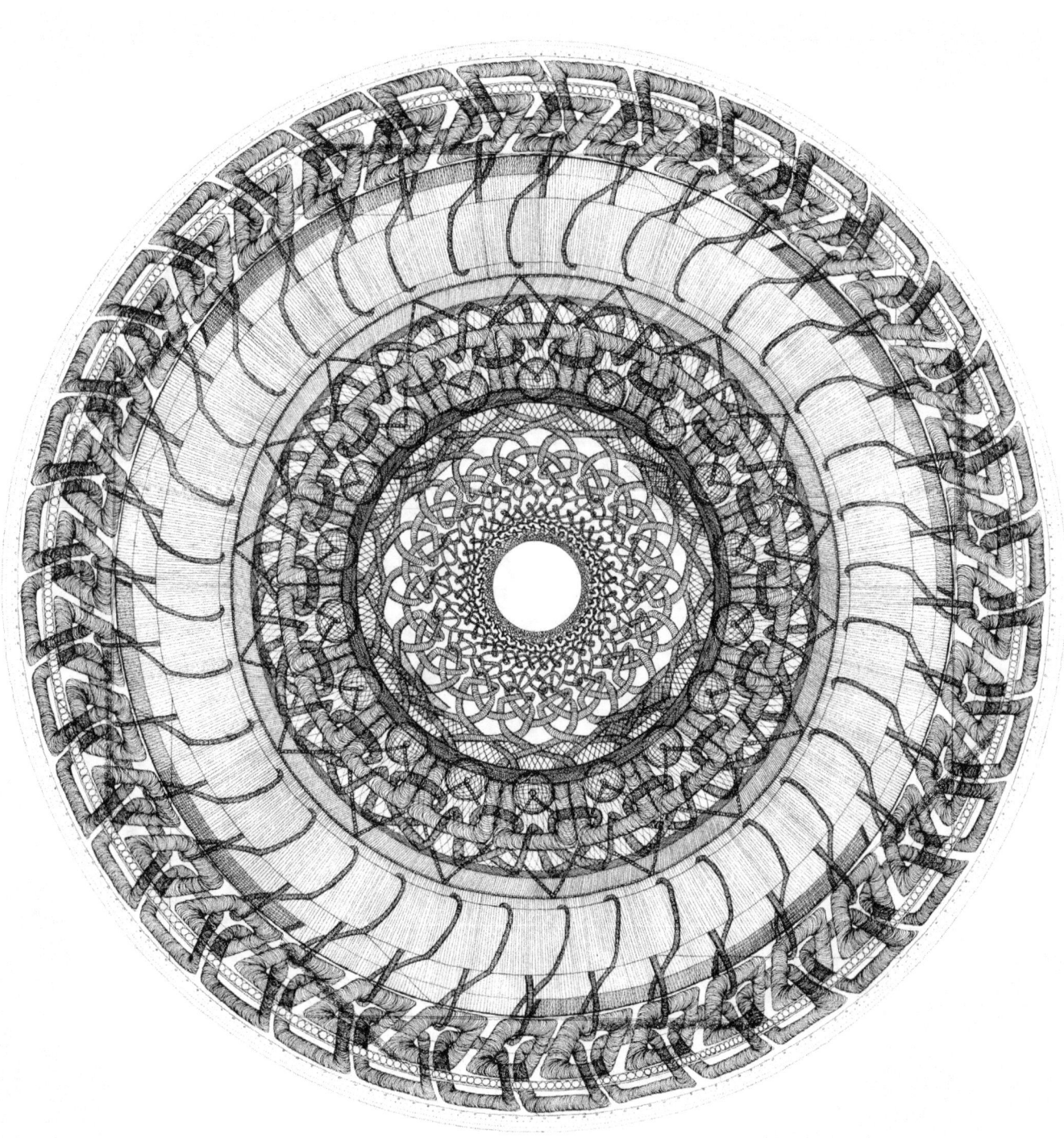

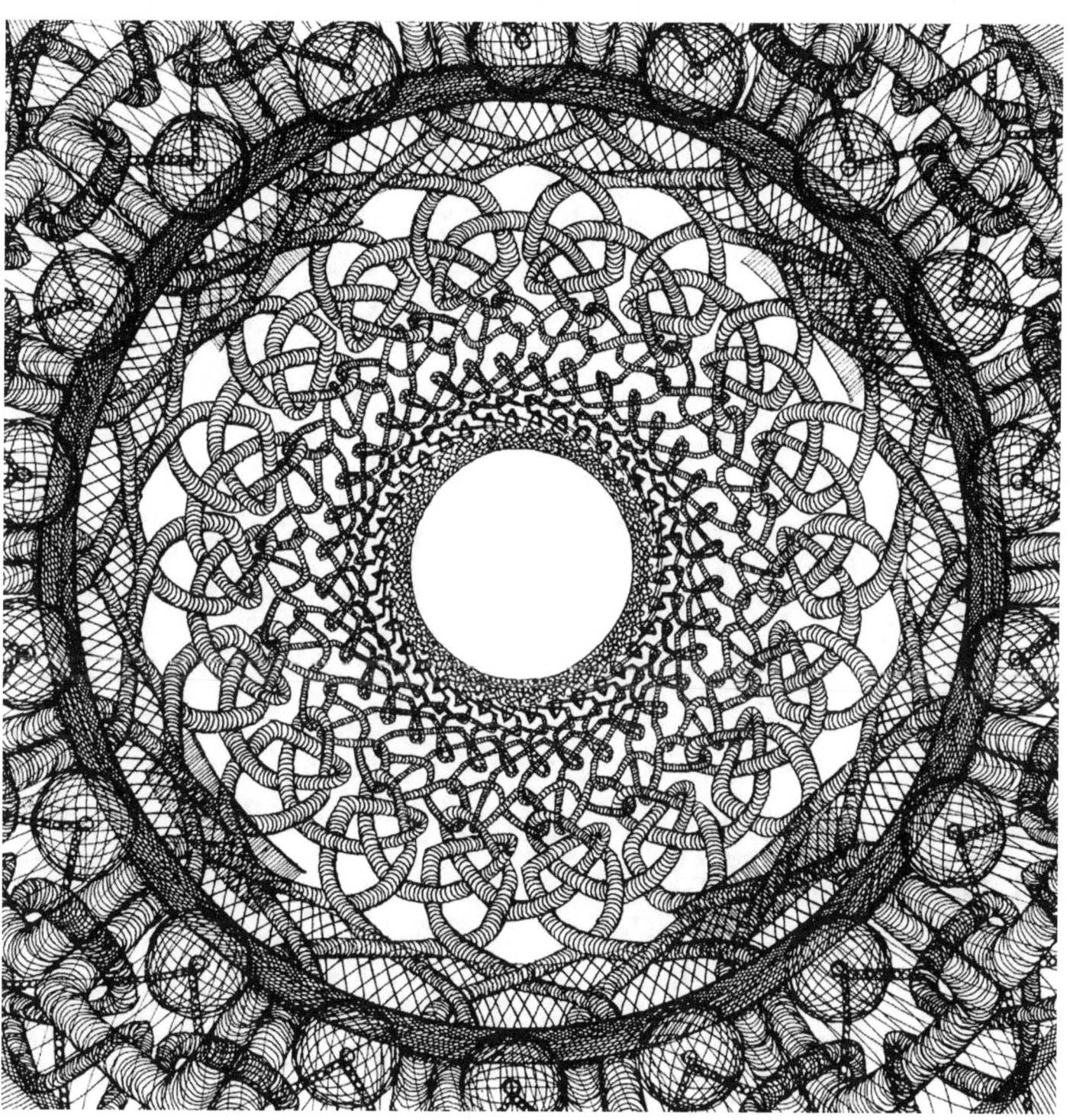

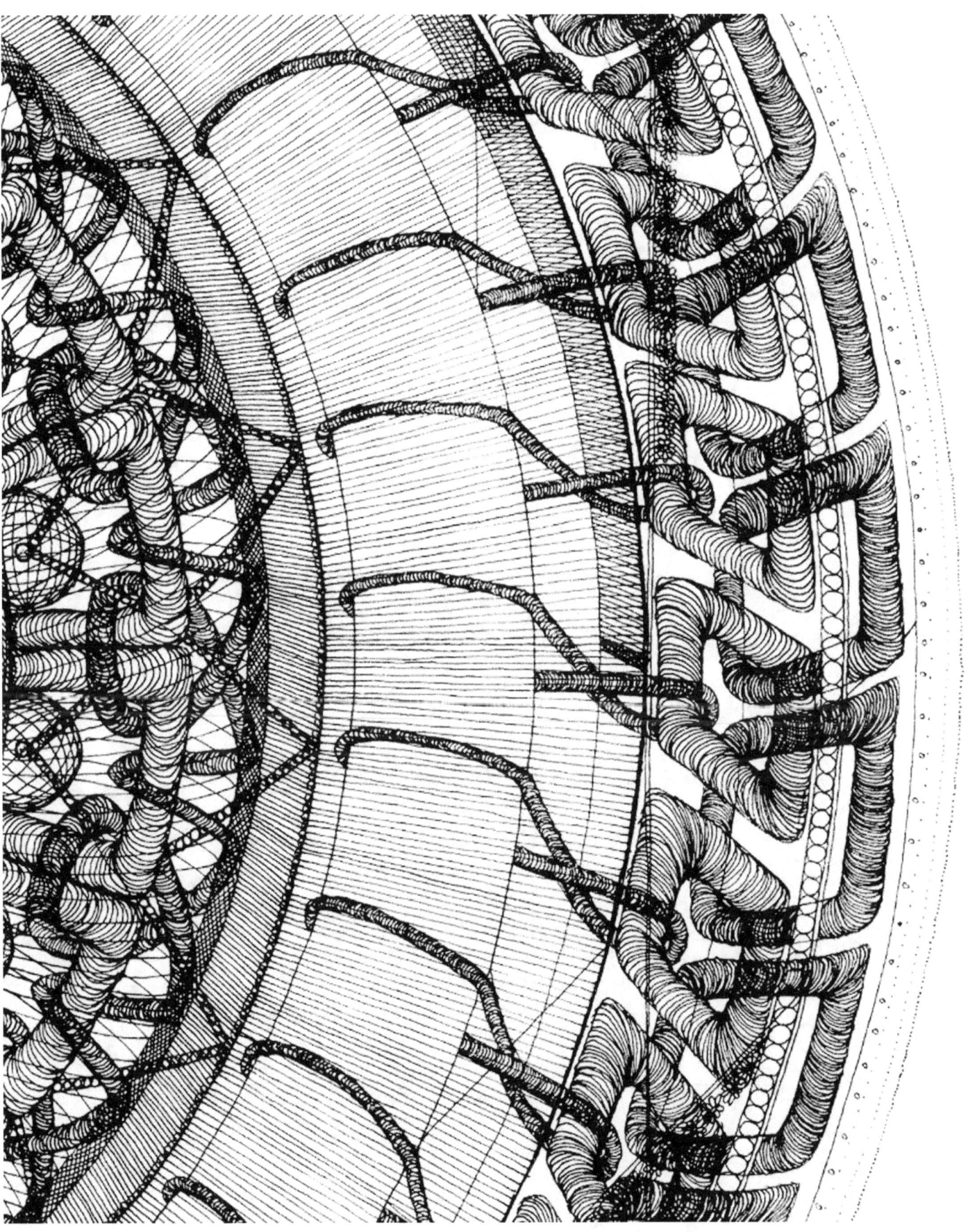

SMALL WHEEL

"It is the harmony of the diverse parts, their symmetry, their happy balance; in a word it is all that introduces order, all that gives unity, that permits us to see clearly and to comprehend at once both the ensemble and the details." ~ Henri Poincare

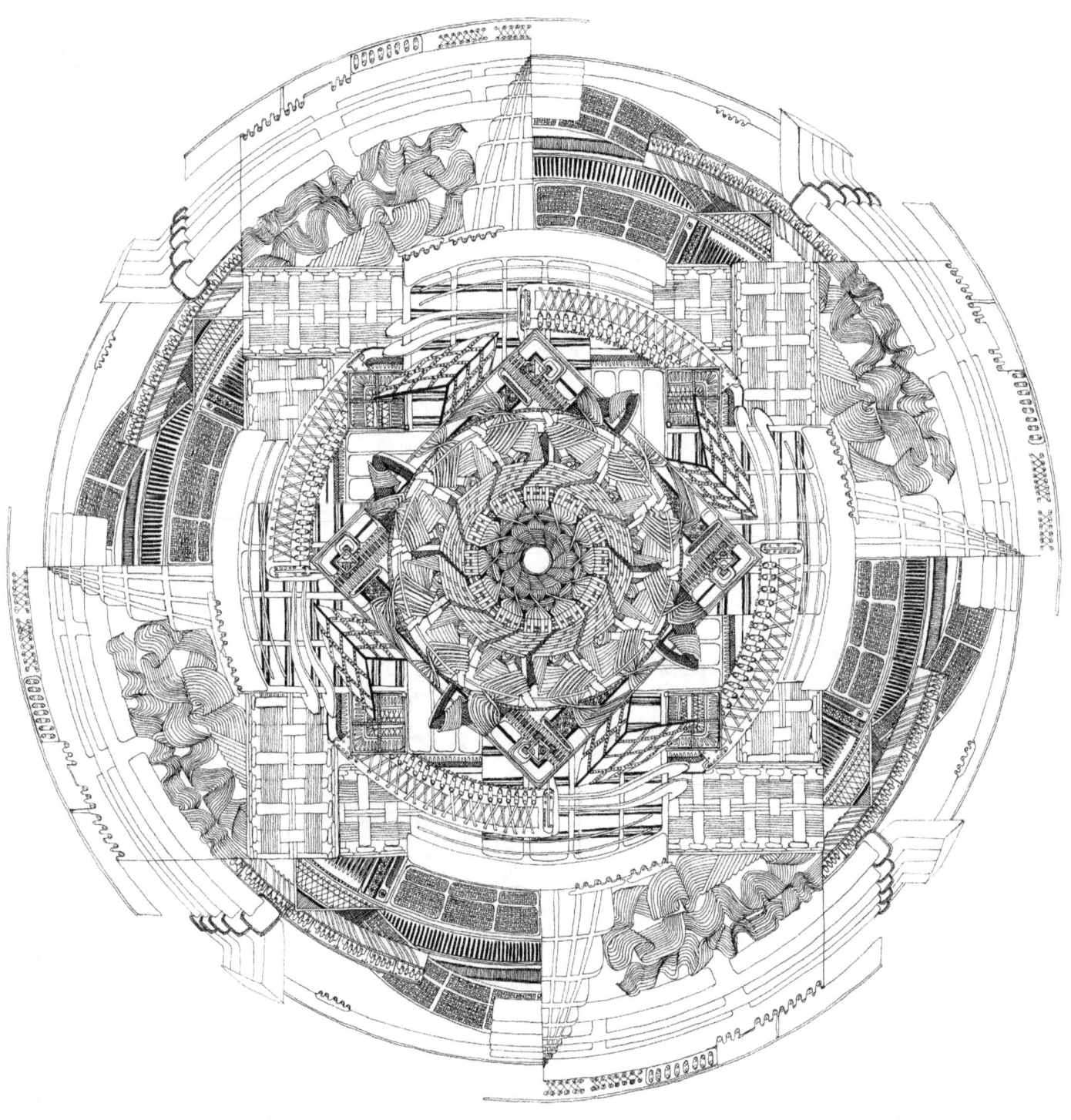

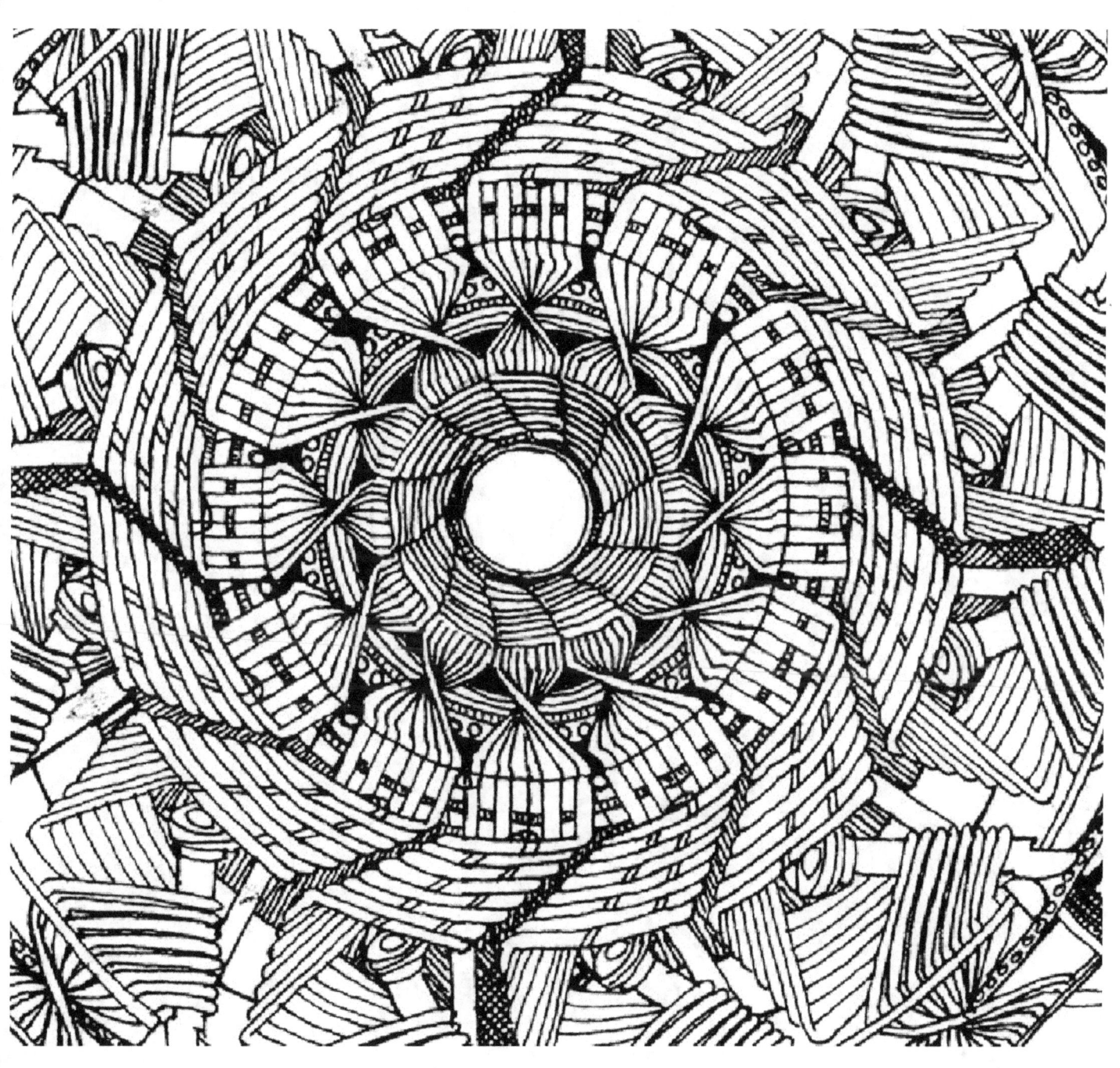

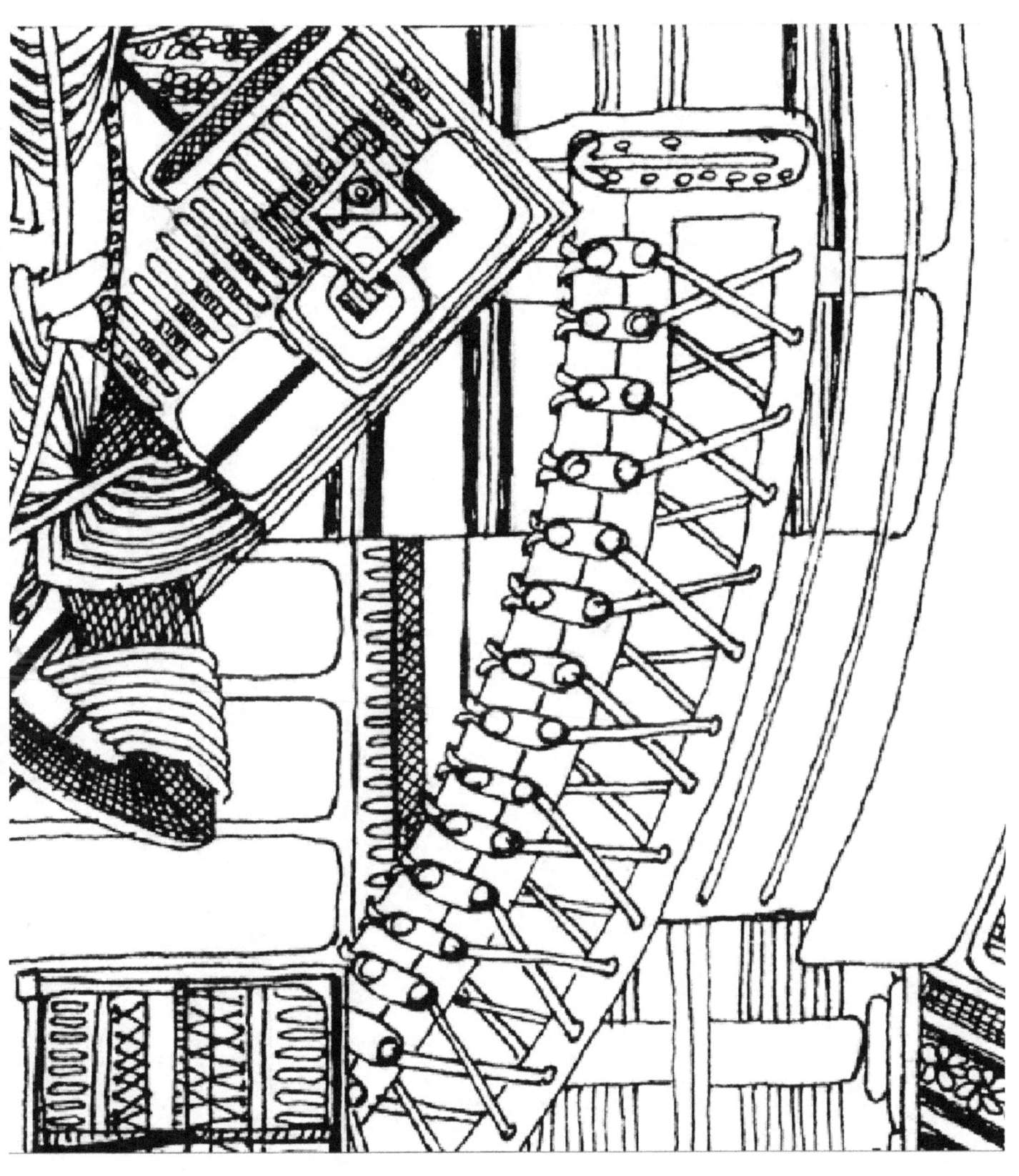

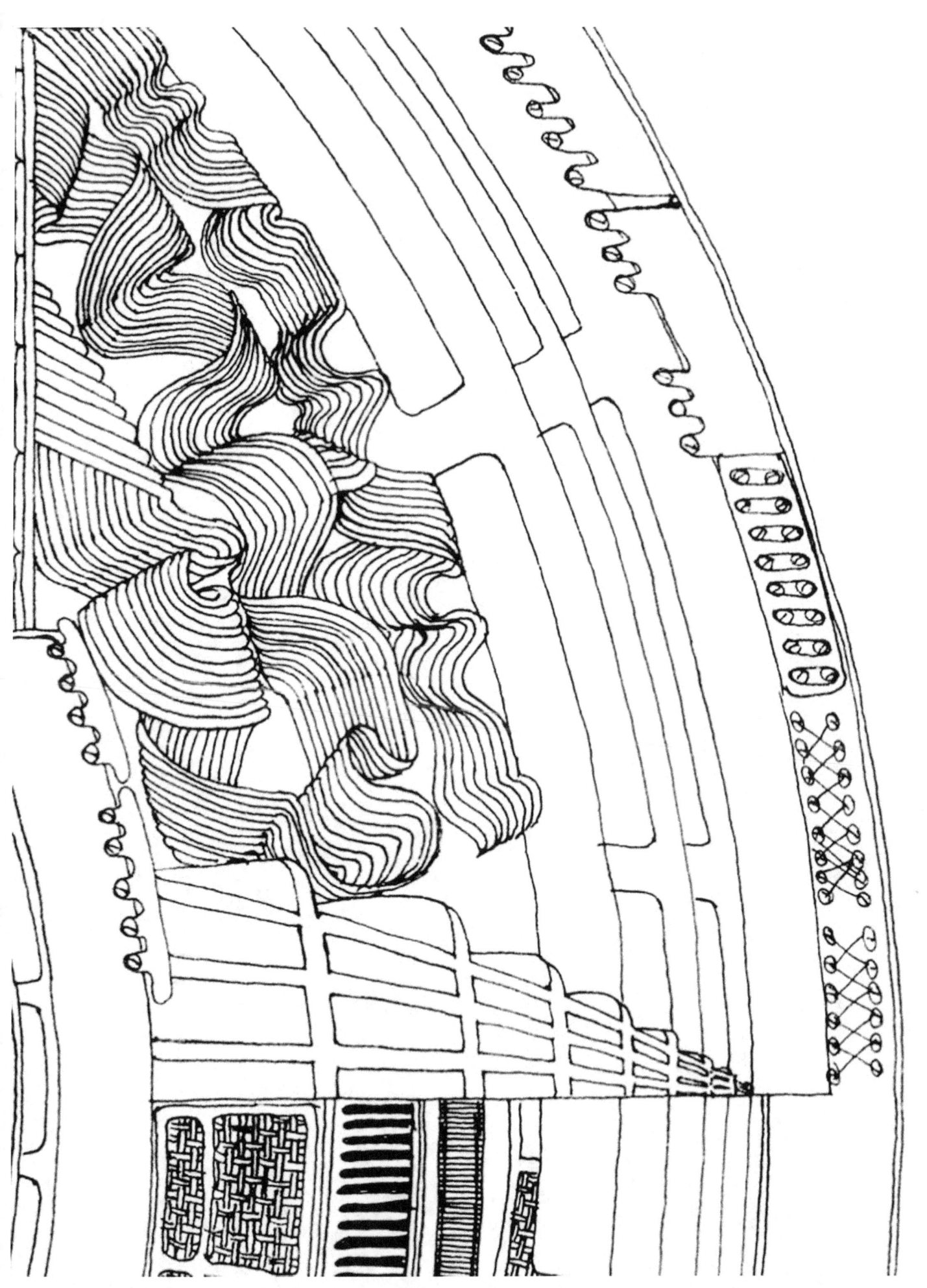

RING

"The nature of God is a circle of which the center is everywhere and the circumference is nowhere."

~ Empedocles

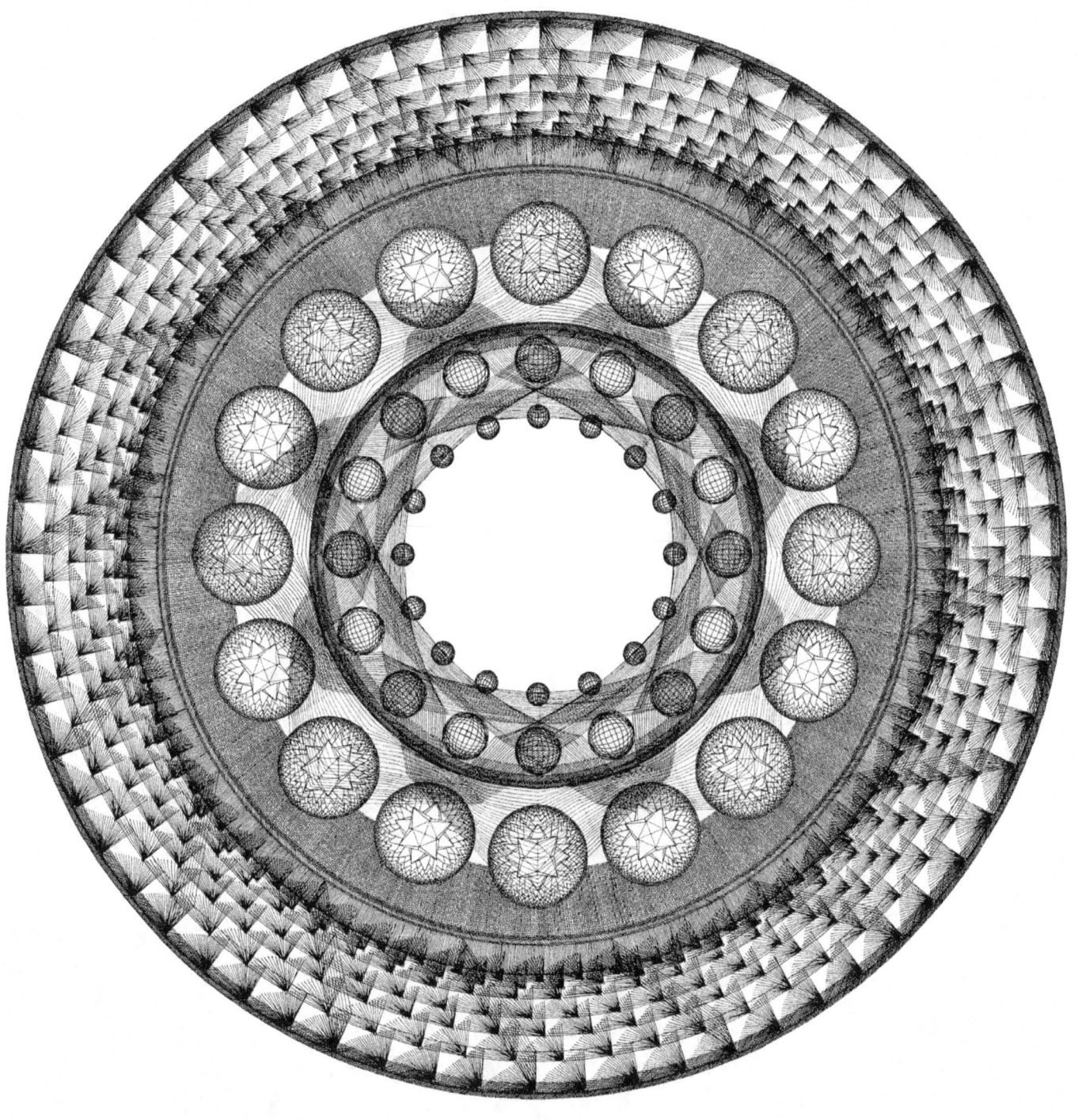

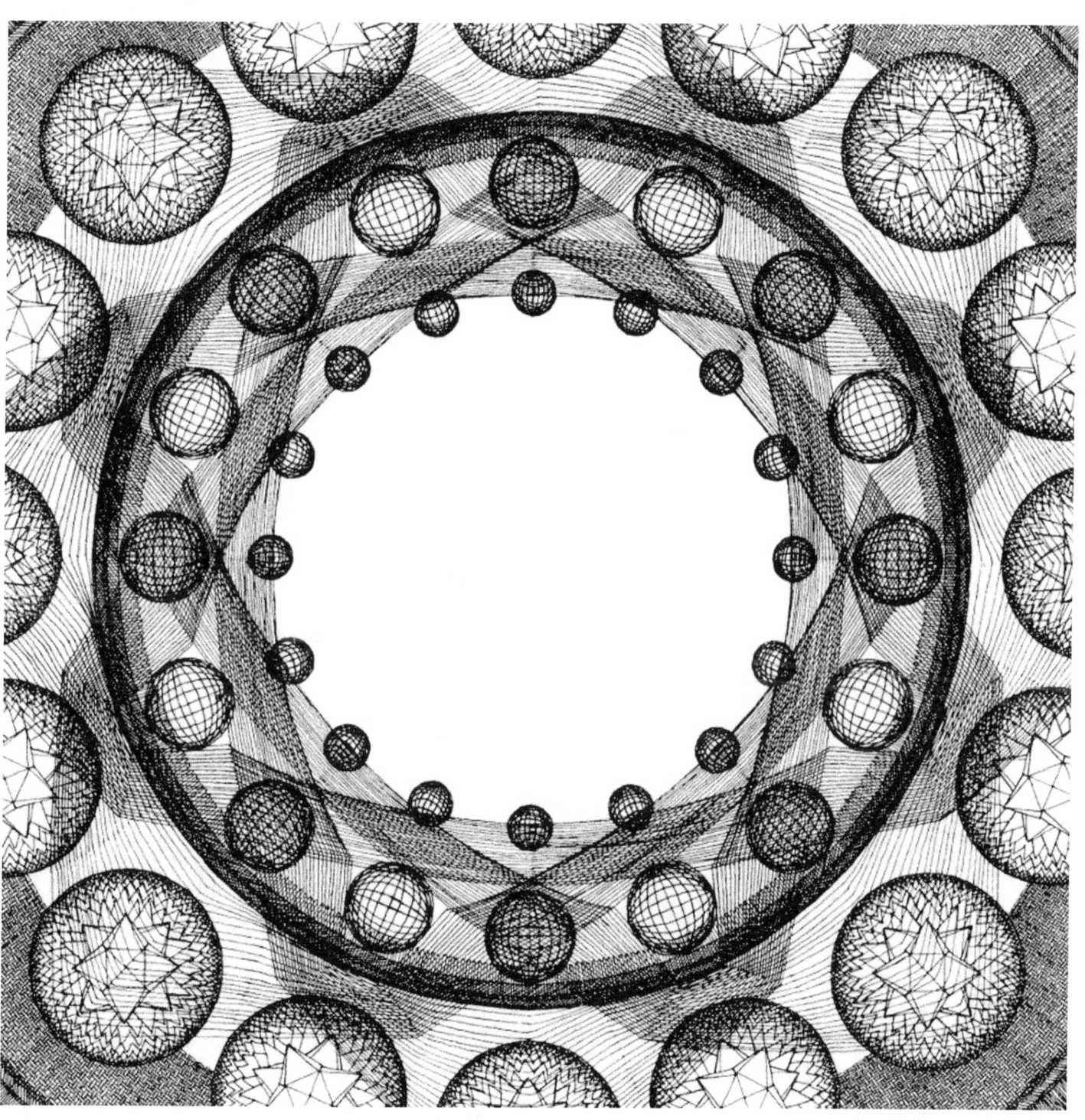

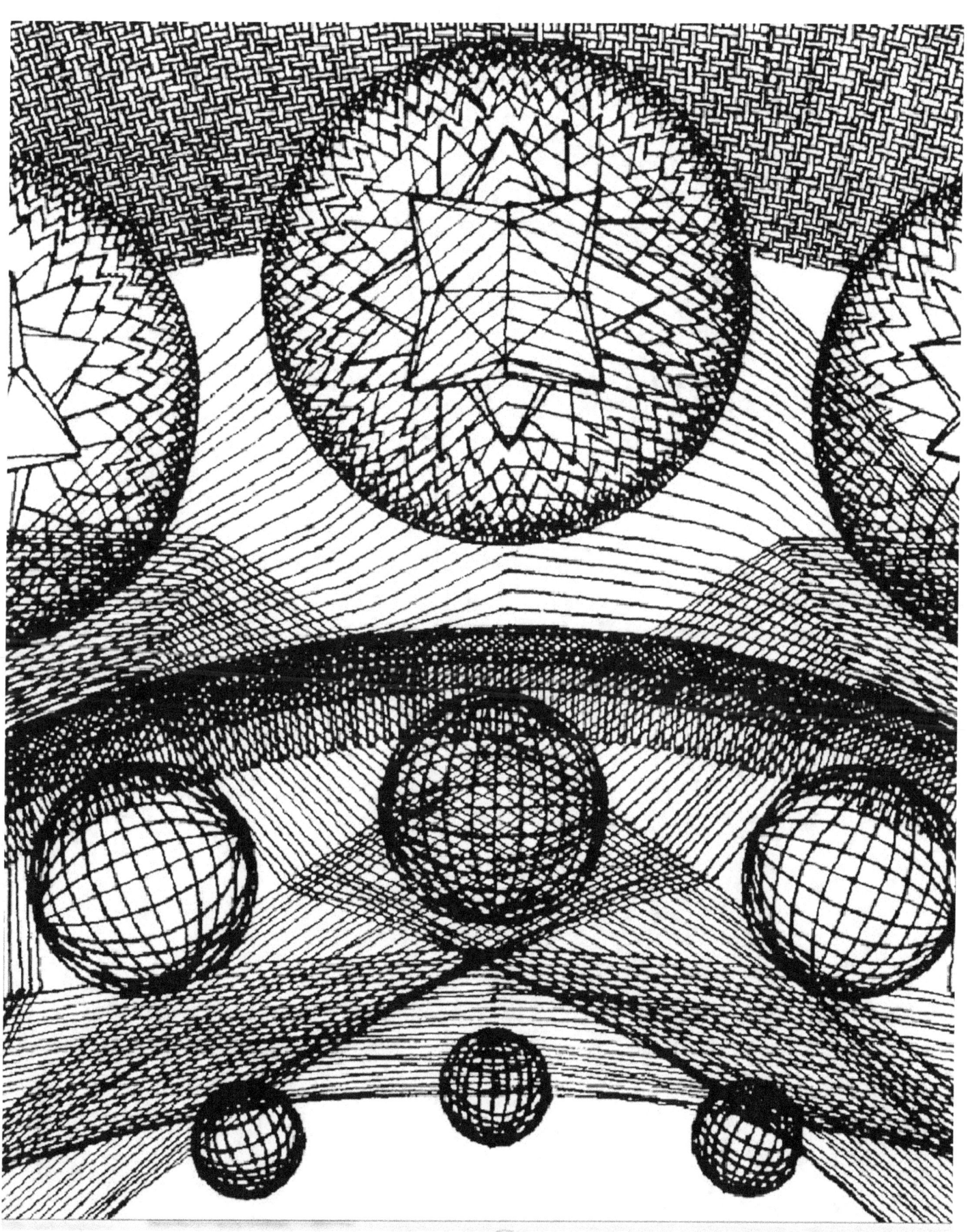

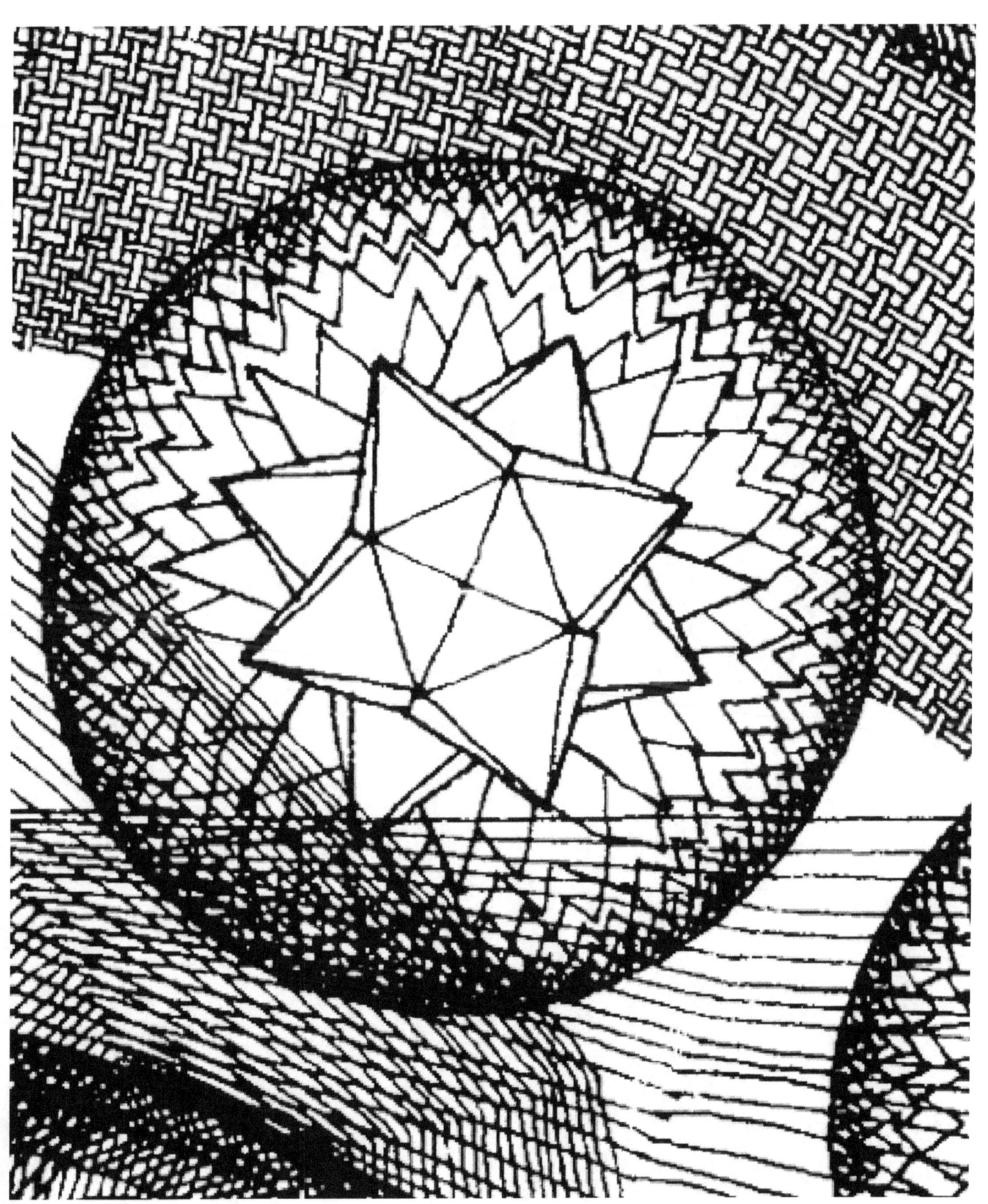

TEST PAGE

Before you get started drawing, try out your pencils, pens and erasers on this page. Look to see if your drawing materials bleed through the back of the page before you start on a drawing you want to keep.

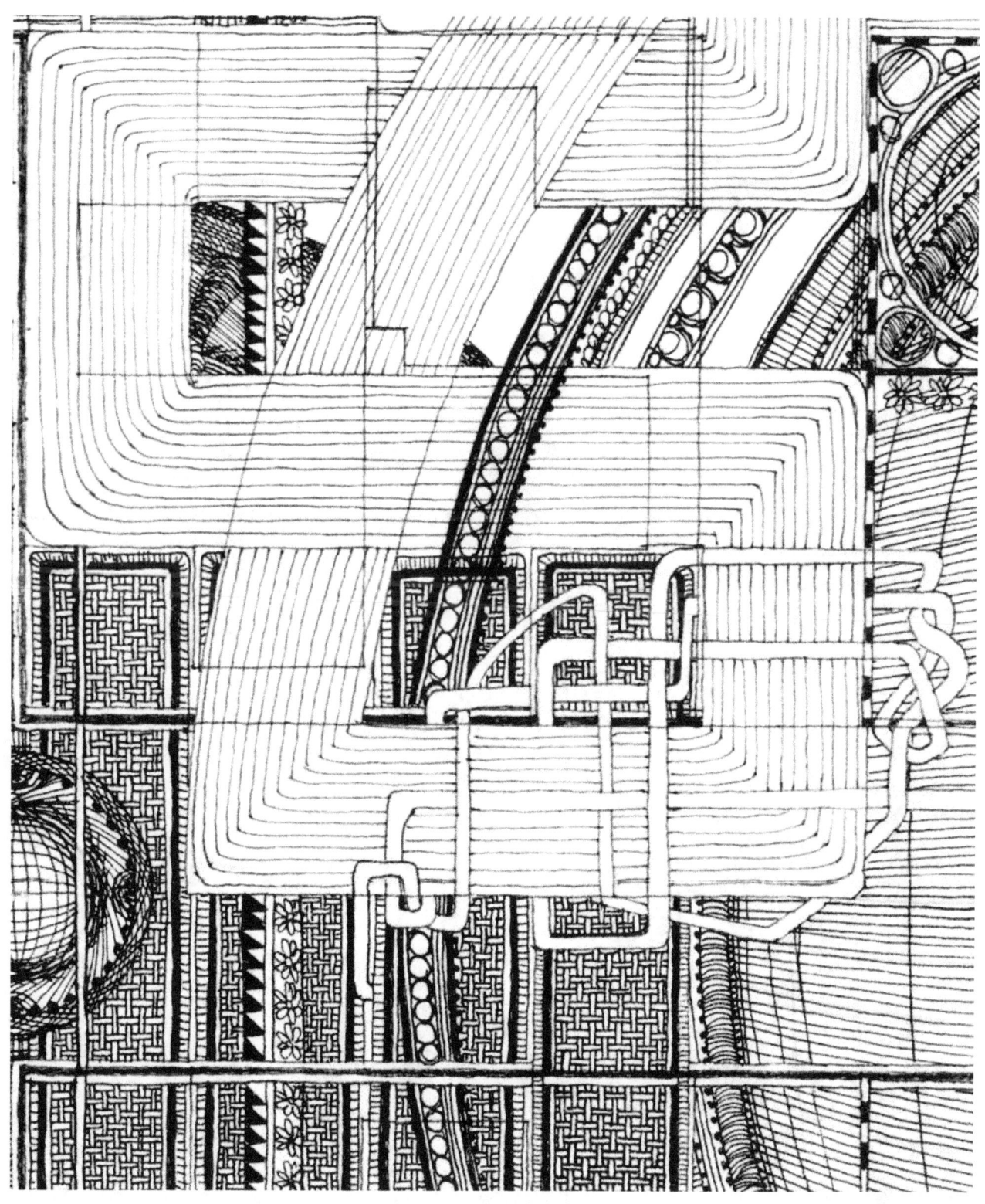

www.ingramcontent.com/pod-product-compliance
Lightning Source LLC
Chambersburg PA
CBHW081017170526
45158CB00010B/3079